ADVENTURE TIME™

FINN & JAKE'S

Am-Ooo-sing
Joke Book

PUFFIN BOOKS

UK | USA | Canada | Ireland | Australia
India | New Zealand | South Africa

Puffin Books is part of the Penguin Random House group of companies whose addresses can be found at global.
penguinrandomhouse.com.

puffinbooks.com

Penguin
Random House
UK

First published 2015
001

With contributions by Ruth Reyes and Adventure Time fans
Text and illustrations copyright ©Cartoon Network, 2015
ADVENTURE TIME, CARTOON NETWORK, the logos, and all related characters and elements
are trademarks of and © Cartoon Network. (s15)
Set in Pendlefont
Printed in Great Britain by Clays Ltd, St Ives plc

A CIP catalogue record for this book is available from the British Library

ISBN: 978–0–141–35770–6

www.greenpenguin.co.uk

Penguin Random House is committed to a
sustainable future for our business, our readers
and our planet. This book is made from Forest
Stewardship Council® certified paper.

ADVENTURE TIME™

FINN & JAKE'S

Am-Ooo-sing
Joke Book

PUFFIN

Contents

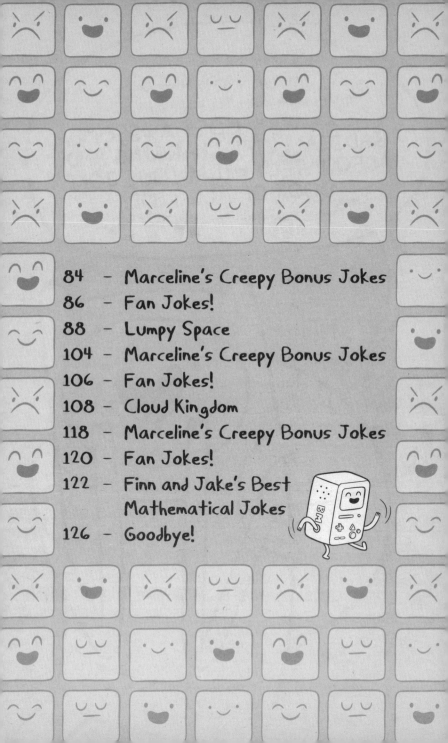

What did Finn's hat say to the rest of Finn's clothes? You stay here, I'll go on a head.

What kind of mathematics does the Cosmic Owl like? Owl-gebra!

There are two slices of bacon in Jake's pan.
One slice turns to the other and says, 'Man, it's hot in here.'
The other slice says, 'What the what? Since when does bacon talk?!'

Jake: Bro, I was surrounded by lions this morning.
Finn: Really? Lions?

Jake: Yeah. Dandelions! HAHAHA.

What is the Never Ending Pie Throwing Robot's favourite planet?
Neptr-tune!

Jake: I'm going to stand outside the Tree Fort.
So, if anyone asks, I'm outstanding!

What does Jake say when he exits the Tree Fort?
I'm leaf-ing!

Why are Jake's bacon pancakes the best? Because they can't be battered!

How does the ocean say hello? It waves.

Finn: I bet I can make you say purple.

Jake: How?

Finn: What colour is Princess Bubblegum?

Jake: Pink.

Finn: I told you I could make you say pink!

Jake: What the huh?! You said purple!

Finn: Ha! Dude, I told you I could make you say purple!

This joke is less funny if you have thalassophobia.

Why is Finn's root sword so awesome? Because it's tree-mendous!

When is a door not a door? When it's a jar.

What's brown and sticky? A stick.

What has a bed you can't sleep in? A river!

What's Jake's favourite thing to put in a burrito? EVERYTHING.

Why did the snail go to the Tree Fort? We don't know. He still hasn't got there!

What would you call it if Shelby took over the world? Global worming!

What kind of room in the Tree Fort can you not go inside? A mushroom!

Why does Finn make other people want to be heroes? Because he's Finn-spirational!

How should you make jokes about the Hot Dog Kingdom? With relish!

What should an adventurer
take on a trip to the desert?
A thirst aid kit!

Why did the squirrel run
round and round in circles?
He'd gone a little nuts!

Why did the monster start
eating candles?
For some light refreshment!

On which days do monsters
like to eat heroes?
Chewsday!

What kind of weapon
grows on the ground?
A blade of grass!

What did BMO say
when he overcharged
his batteries?

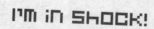

I'm in Shock!

What did the
beaver say to
the Tree Fort?
It's been nice
gnawing you.

What did the
Tree Fort say
when all its
leaves fell off?
I don't be-leaf it!

Why did the Tree Fort
go to the doctor?
Because it had a
window pane.

What's BMO's favourite kind of snack?
Computer chips!

What does the Tree Fort have in common with an elephant?
They both have trunks!

What's the best thing to put in an apple pie baked by Tree Trunks?
Your teeth!

Finn: Knock, knock!

Jake: Who's there?

Finn: Orange.

Jake: Orange who?

Finn: Orange you going to let me in, man?!

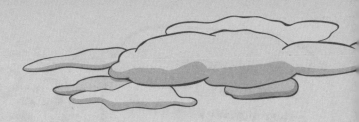

What kind of rocks are never found in the ocean?
Dry ones.

How does the Tree Witch get around?
She witch-hikes!

What do you call a man in a hole?
Doug!

What do you call a man overlooking the ocean?
Cliff!

Why does Banana Man wear suntan lotion? Because otherwise he'd peel!

How do you catch a squirrel? Climb a tree and act like a nut!

How do you send a message in the forest? By moss code.

What does Finn call the end of a heroic battle? The Finnale!

If you drop your sword in the mud, what will you get out? A dirty sword. Duh.

Jake: Knock, knock!
Finn: Who's there?

Jake: Bark!
Finn: Bark who?

Jake: I'm barking
because I'm a dog.

What do you
call Jake when
he gets angry?
Barking mad!

What's the most
lethal part of any joke?
The punchline.

Jake: Hey, Finn. What kind
of cheese isn't yours?
Finn: I don't know, dude.

Jake: NACHO CHEESE!

Why did Finn throw food on Jake?
Because Jake said, "Dinner is on me!"

What do you call the Snail without his shell?
Homeless!

Finn: Knock, knock!
Jake: Who's there?
Finn: Boo!
Jake: Boo who?
Finn: Hey, man, don't cry! It's only me!

What drink would a hero give an evil monster?
Fruit PUNCH!

Marceline's Creepy Bonus Jokes

What's red, red and red all over?
Don't know but it sounds delicious!

What do you call a vampire who's totally lost it?
Batty!

Why don't skeletons fight each other?
Because they don't have the guts!

Why can't skeletons play music?
Because they don't have organs.

What do you call two witches who live together?
Broom-mates.

What soup do vampires eat?
Alpha-BAT soup.

Why did I throw the clock out of the window?
To see time fly — like me!

What kind of letters do vampires get?
Fang mail!

What's a vampire's favourite fruit?
Neck-tarines!

FAN JOKES

Did you hear about the goblin
who injured his ankle?
He was a hobblin' goblin!

Daniel

Why was six
scared of seven?
Because seven
eight nine!

Daisy

What do you call a
cow that eats grass?
A lawn-mooer!

Isabella

Jake: Dude, how was your camping trip?
Finn: It was okay, but I got badly bitten.
Jake: Didn't you take a mosquito net?
Finn: Yeah, but it didn't put the vampires off!

Jack

Why were there no red
crayons in the crayon box?
Because Marceline got hungry.

Sophie

What do you call a kid that neighs?
Naked!

Samuel

Knock, knock!
Who's there?
BMO.
BMO who?
BMO best friend!

Anna

Why do the trees in the Evil Forest hate maths?
Because it gives them square roots.

Zoey

Jake: Why're you doing your multiplication on the floor?
Finn: Because you said not to use tables!

Robert

What happens if you cross Toast Princess and Hotdog Princess?
A royal feast!

Joel

27

What happened to the Ice King when all the princesses escaped? He had a meltdown!

What did the Ice King say before beginning his comedy routine? This is gonna sleigh you!

Why doesn't the Ice King need to sleep much? Because he's always kid-napping!

What do Snow Golems eat for lunch? Iceberg-ers.

What do you call
Gunter when it's in
the Fire Kingdom?
Lost!

What do you get
when you cross
Marceline and a
Snow Golem?
Frostbite.

What's black and white and black
and white and black and white?
Gunter rolling down a mountain.

What's the
Ice King's
favourite
snack?
Brrrr-itos.

What's black and white and pink
and black and white and pink?
Gunthalina rolling down a mountain.

What's black and white
and red all over?
Gunter with a sunburn.

Why do princesses
not want to marry
the Ice King?
Because he treats
them so coldly!

What do you call an ice
palace in a heatwave?
A puddle!

What was the Ice King's favourite part of school?
Snow and tell!

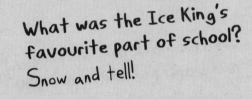

Finn: Knock, knock!
Ice King: Who's there?
Finn: Harry.
Ice King: Harry who?
Finn: Harry up and let us in, it's freezing out here!

What do the Snow Men call their offspring?
Chilly-dren.

How do Snow Golems get to work?
By icicle!

How do you keep from getting cold feet in the Ice Kingdom?
Don't go brrrr-footed!

What's the Ice King's favourite cake topping?
Frosting!

Ice King: Knock, knock!
Princess Bubblegum: Who's there?
Ice King: Olive!
Princess Bubblegum: Olive who?
Ice King: Olive you, Princess! JUST MARRY ME ALREADY!

Why doesn't the Ice Palace get cold in the winter?
Because it wears a snowcap!

Why is Ricardio the Heart Guy great at playing music?
Because he always has a good beat!

What's black and white and goes round and round?
Gunter in a revolving door.

What do the penguins make their beds with?
Sheets of ice and blankets of snow!

What do you get if you cross
Ice King with his drum kit?
Cool music!

What does the Ice King say
to his kidnapped princesses?
Have an ice day!

Why did the Ice King put
his money in the freezer?
He wanted cold hard cash!

What do you call it when
Kitten helps Gunter take
over the Land of Ooo?
A cat-astrophe!

What's black and white
and has eight wheels?
Gunter on roller skates.

What's the biggest
problem with snow boots?
They melt!

Jake: Knock, knock!
Ice King: Who's there?
Jake: Ivor.
Ice King: Ivor who?
Jake: Ivor you let us in,
Ice King, or we're climbing
through the window!

How do Gunter and
the penguins drink?
Out of their beak-ers!

Why was Ice King sad?
He felt ice-olated!

What did the penguins sing at the Ice King's birthday?
Freeze a jolly good fellow!

What did the Ice King say to the escaping princess?
Freeze!

What do you call an angry Ice-o-Pede?
You don't call him anything — you just run!

What does a Snow Golem like for breakfast?
Snowflakes.

Finn: Knock, knock!
Ice King: Who's there?
Finn: Snow.
Ice King: Snow who?
Finn: Snowbody! Hahaha, FOOLED YOU.

Why did the Snow Golem throw his computer away? It kept freezing up!

What does the Ice King get when he meets a princess? A frosty reception!

What is an Ice-o-Pede's favourite cake? Any cake, as long as there is ice-ing.

When is snow not snow?
When it's adrift!

What shoes does Ice King
wear around the Ice Palace?
Slippers.

How do Gunter and the
penguins make decisions?
They flipper coin!

What does the
Ice King take
when he's ill?
A chill pill.

What
kind of
parties do
they have in
the Ice Kingdom?
Snowballs!

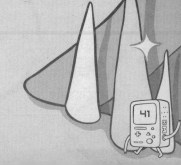

Jake: Knock, knock!
Ice King: Who's there?
Jake: Emma!
Ice King: Emma who?
Jake: Emma bit cold out here, man . . . let me in!

Why do the penguins have thick layers of feathers?
Because it's snow cold!

What do you call a forgetful snowman?
Flaky.

What is the Ice King's favourite song?
There's snow business like snow-business!

Why can't you tell a joke in the Ice Kingdom? Because the ice might crack up!

How is a drum kit different to Finn and Jake? The Ice King can only beat his drum kit!

Why was the ice storm so fast? It was sleet of foot!

Why was the blizzard so thick? Because it had snow idea what it was talking about.

Marceline's Creepy Bonus Jokes

Why are there fences around cemeteries?
Because people are dying to get in!

What's a scaredycat's favourite dessert?
I-scream.

How does a vampire queen
keep her hair in place?
With scare-spray!

Where do baby ghosts
go during the day?
Dayscare centres!

Where do ghosts mail
their letters?
At the ghost office.

What do you call a
vampire who referees
a tennis match?
A vumpire!

What's it like
when a vampire has
a crush on you?
A pain in the neck!

Where do ghosts buy their food?
At the ghost-ery store!

What do you get if you cross a
two-headed duck with a vampire?
Two Count Quackulas!

FAN JOKES

What did Gunter decorate his birthday cake with?
Chocolate Ice-king!

Jon

Jake: Dude, I feel like a pair of curtains . . .
Finn: Pull yourself together, man!

Kamila

What's Ice King's favourite salad?
Iceberg lettuce.

Charlotte

Why do Ice King's plans always fail?
Because he gets cold feet!

Eoife

What does Marceline have at eleven o'clock every day?
A coffin break.

Rhys

Why does Gunter carry fish in his beak?
Because he hasn't got any pockets.

Dylan

How does Ice King build
a house with snow?
Igloo-s it!

Madison

What falls
down but never
gets hurt?
Snow!

Angelina

What do snowmen say
when they melt?
Freezey come, freezey go!

Natalie

What's worse than biting into
an apple and finding Shelby in it?
Biting into an apple and finding the
Ice King in it!

Joel

47

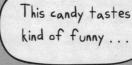

What kind of candy should you eat in space?
Flying saucers.

What do you call a rabbit dressed up as cake?
A cream bun!

How does Princess Bubblegum freshen her breath in the lab?
With experi-mints!

What kind of candy has no teeth?
A gummy bear!

Why did the Banana Guard go to the doctor? Because he wasn't peeling well.

Why did Mr Cupcake
go to the Ice Kingdom?
To top up his frost-ing!

Finn: Knock, knock!
Jake: Who's there?
Finn: Doughnut.
Jake: Doughnut who?
Finn: Doughnut ask, bro . . .
it's a SECRET.

Where does Peppermint
Butler keep his photos?
On his mint-lepiece.

How did Princess Bubblegum's perfect sandwich taste? Loaf-ly and dough-lightful!

Why is a Candy Person's hair so sticky? Because they use a honeycomb!

What's the best way to clean your teeth in the Candy Kingdom? With candyfloss.

Why did Cinnamon Bun stop looking at his body? He'd had it with the hole thing!

Why did the Gingerbread Man go to the doctor?
Because he was feeling crumby.

What do you give the Earl of Lemongrab when he's ill?
Lemon-aid.

What kind of street do Candy Zombies like best?
A dead end!

Finn: Did you hear about the pancake stack that got mad?
Jake: Yeah, it totally flipped!

How often does Princess Bubblegum look at her table of elements? Periodically!

Where do Candy People learn to make desserts? In sundae school!

Why did Lemongrab like Lemongrab 2 so much? Because he found him a-peeling!

What's rainbow-coloured and flies really fast? Lady Rainicorn when she's in a rush!

Why did Dr Doughnut
go to the dentist?
He needed a chocolate filling.

What did the fillings in PB's perfect
sandwich say to each other?
Lettuce get together!

What wobbles
as it flies?
A jelly-copter!

What
do you
call elderly
Jelly Bean
People?
Has-beans!

What did the icing
say to the bun?
I've got you covered!

Why did Princess Bubblegum remove
the doorbell from her lab door?
She wanted to win the no-bell prize!

Why couldn't Dr Doughnut
eat his lunch?
He was already stuffed.

Why did Finn sleep with
candy under his pillow?
He wanted sweet dreams.

Why was Chocoberry the strawberry sad?
Because her mother was in a jam!

What do you call it when you're trapped in the Cotton Candy Forest?
A sticky situation!

Why did Finn mess with Princess Bubblegum's chemistry experiment?
To see if he could get a reaction!

Why are the Marshmallow Kids always kind to everyone?
Because they're such softies.

What do Root Beer Guy's detective story and Mr Cupcake have in common? They've both got a case!

What tastes better than Princess Bubblegum's Royal tarts? NOTHING!!!

What kind of cookie makes you rich? A fortune cookie!

What's white and fluffy and lives in a tree? A meringue-utan.

Which Candy Person has most in common with a tree?
ROOT Beer Guy!

Why did Lemongrab stop running around?
He'd run out of juice!

Why did LSP want a job in a bakery?
So she could loaf around!

What's Princess Bubblegum's favourite way to get around?
On a chew-chew train!

What is a ghost's favourite candy? Boo-ble gum!

What kind of candy is always late? Choco-late!

How do scientists make friends at PB's Science Barbecues? They give each other a good grilling!

What do you get when an apple pie goes for a run? Puff pastry!

Why are Banana Guards never lonely? Because they hang out in bunches!

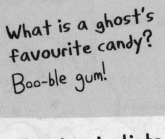

What do you call it when PB runs from one side of her lab to the other?
A Petri dash!

What does Lady Rainicorn like to wear in her hair?
A rain-bow.

How do you describe Pineapple Guy when he's in a bad mood?
Spiky!

Why was the gingerbread couple sad?
Because they broke up.

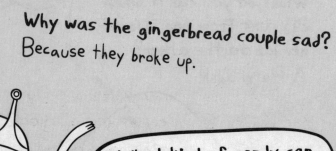

What kind of candy can you make clothes with?
Cotton candy!

What did Mr Cupcake say when he got squashed?
Crumbs!

What's Starchie's favourite kind of party?
A chocolate malt ball!

Marceline's Creepy Bonus Jokes

What do I call it when there's no red around for me to eat?
Red-iculous!

What does a ghost call his mum or dad?
TransPARENT!

Who would win a war between the vampires and the skeletons?
Nobody – it would be DEAD even!

What's the worst day of the week for a vampire?
Sun-day!

How many tickles does it take
to make a slimy monster laugh?
Ten-tickles!

Why couldn't Princess
Beautiful laugh at my
awesome jokes?
She lost her funny bone.

How do you describe a
vampire's attitude?
We have bat tempers!

What would my cool
vampire friends say
about these jokes?
"They SUCK."

What kind of
horses only go
out at night?
Night-mares.

FAN JOKES

What would you get if you mashed Princess Bubblegum and Jake together?
A PB & J sandwich!

Evan

What do you call someone who leaves the Candy Kingdom forever?
A dessert-er!

Gerry

So, do you wanna hear the rad joke about Jake's arms?
Actually, forget it. It kinda stretches on a bit . . .

Toby

Where does Princess Bubblegum like to go on vacation?
Finn-land!

Mia

What does the sun drink out of?
Sunglasses.

Mikey

What's the difference
between a piano and tuna?
You can tune a piano but you
can't piano tuna!

Annie

What's Princess Bubblegum's
favourite sugary substance?
Not sherbet I can ask her for you!

Lucas

What do you do
when life gives
you lemons?
Do NOT make
a Lemongrab!

Hoseph

Why did the
Candy child cry?
Because his
mother had been
a wafer so long.

Thomas

What do you call
Dr Ice Cream in his car?
A sundae driver.

Riley

What do you call an attractive Flame Person?
Lava-ble!

Which legend of the Fire Kingdom really likes maths?
Fire Count!

What kind of crackers does Flame Princess like to eat?
Fire crackers!

What kind of balls does Flame Princess like to attend?
Fireballs!

Why is Flame King a terrible chef?
He burns EVERYTHING.

What happened to
Flame Princess and
Finn's spark?
He blew it.

Who invented fire?
Some bright spark.

Which is faster: heat or cold?
Heat, because you can catch a cold!

What did Mr Pig say
after spending a day
in the Fire Kingdom?

I'm bacon!

Why is everyone in the Fire Kingdom so angry all the time? Because they're so hot-headed!

Why else are the Flame People so angry? Because their blood is always boiling!

Did you hear about the fire at the circus? The heat was in tents!

What do you call it when Flame Princess attacks the Ice King's palace? A meltdown!

How do you make fire
with two sticks?
Make sure one is a match!

What only
starts to work
after it's fired?
A rocket!

What did the
Lava Man say to
the Lava Woman?
I lava you.

What do you call
Jalapeño Pepper when
he's being nosy?
Jalapeño business!

How would Flame Princess describe
her magical scented candles?
Scent-sational!

What's the quickest way to make a Flame Guard mad at you?
Call him a candelabra.

What do you call an extra tall, extra mean-looking Flame Guard?
Sir!

Why can't you ever have ice cream in the Fire Kingdom?
Because it will melt. DUH.

What kind of food does Jalapeño Pepper like to cook?
Anything flame-grilled.

What's worse than being chased by a pack of wolves?
Being chased by a pack of Fire Wolves.

What does a Lava Man call his mother?
Mag-Ma!

What do you call a Snow Golem who makes friends with a Fire Wolf?
Water!

What do you call Jake when he's in the Fire Kingdom?
A hot dog.

What was Flame Princess and Finn's favourite song when they were a couple?
Burnin' Love!

What happens when a Flame Person gets embarrassed?
They feel ash-amed.

What's the best way to pet a Fire Wolf?
NEVER PET A FIRE WOLF.

Unless you're happy to say goodbye to your hands.

What two seasons are there in the Fire Kingdom?
Hot . . . and Hotter!

What does Jalapeño Pepper
do when he's angry?
He gets jalapeño face!

What's hotter than the
surface of the sun?
Flame Princess's temper.
Ouch.

Why did the dragon
breathe fire?
Because he swallowed
the Flame King!

What comes out
of taps in the
Fire Kingdom?
Steam!

What happened when
Flame King ran really far?
He felt burned out!

What do you get if you cross Flame
Princess with a glass of water?
Steaming rage!

What does a
Lava Man wash
himself with?
Molten lather!

What's the least scary way
to describe a volcano?
Call it a mountain with hiccups.

What kind of
temper does Flame
Princess have?
A fiery one!

How do the Flame
People stay cool?
THEY DON'T.

What do you call Cinnamon
Bun after he's spent time
in the Fire Kingdom?
Fully baked.

What happens when you cross a Flame Person with dynamite?
An explosion!

What do you call grass that's been stepped on by a Lava Man?
Dead!

What happens when a Flame Person falls in love?
Sparks fly.

What's another name for the Fire Kingdom throne?
The hot seat.

What happens when Colonel Candy Corn goes to the Fire Kingdom?
He becomes Colonel Popcorn!

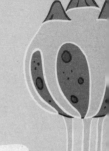

What do you call the Flame King in his lantern, after the sun goes down? A night light!

What currency do Flame People use? C-ash!

What does a Flame Person shout when they see something amazing? Unbe-lava-able!

Why didn't it work out between Finn and Flame Princess? He was too cool for her!

Marceline's Creepy Bonus Jokes

Why did the Skeleton Guard go to the Science Barbecue?
To get a spare rib!

What's my favourite way to get in touch with people?
To f-axe them!

How does a vampire describe something awesome?
Fang-tastic.

Why do ghosts make good cheerleaders?
Because they have a lot of spirit!

What's a monster's favourite fruit?
Boo-berries!

How do monsters like their eggs?
Terror-fried.

What do you call it when I play bass so good that a building collapses?
An axe-ident.

What do ghosts eat for dinner?
Spook-etti!

What's a mummy's favourite kind of music?
Rap!

FAN JOKES

What did Finn say
to Flame Princess?
You're hot!

Kieran

Did you hear about the Flame
People that got married?
They're a match made in heaven!

Sanne

What's the world's
strongest bird?
A crane.

Dominic

What do you call
a surgeon with
eight arms?
A doctor-pus!

Tyler

Why didn't the ghost want to go
to his maths class?
Because he was too ghoul for school.

David

What is a zombie's favourite kind of tree?

A ceme-tree.

Abigail

What's Marceline's favourite bit of a magazine?

The horror-scopes!

Grace

Did you hear about the plastic surgeon who got too close to the fire?

He melted!

Niomi

How do Flame Princess and Cinammon Bun get on?

Like a house on fire!

Kingsley

What do you call a boomerang that won't come back?

A stick.

Luke

How do you organize a Lumpy Space party? You planet!

What's smooth and round in Lumpy Space? LOSERS.

Why does LSP look down on Brad? Because she's SO OVER him.

What's it like travelling through a frog's mouth into Lumpy Space? Toad-ally crazy!

LSP: Knock, knock!
Finn: Who's there?

LSP: Celeste.
Finn: Celeste who?

LSP: Celeste time I'm going to tell you a knock-knock joke.

Why did the Lumpy Space Person want to leave the party?
The atmosphere wasn't right.

What do LSP and gone-off milk have in common?
They're both spoiled and lumpy!

Finn: Hey, LSP, tell me a joke!
Lumpy Space Princess: YOUR FACE IS A JOKE.

Why was Glasses feeling embarrassed?
He made a spectacle of himself.

LSP: Hey, Finn.
What kind of bomb
is the best kind?
Finn: Ummm . . . no kind?
LSP: A DRAMA BOMB!

What's the best way for
a Lumpy Space guy to
impress a regular girl?
By being smooth!

LSP: Finn, I'm hard core. I once lived on
a tin of beans for weeks!
Finn: Weren't you afraid of falling off?

Brad: Hey, LSP, do you know why you need a stepladder?
LSP: No. Why?
Brad: TO GET OVER ME.

What does LSP think is cooler than Promcoming? NOTHING. Duh.

Why did the cow go up into space? To see a mooooon!

What do you call a Lumpy Space King with three eyes? A Lumpy Space Kiiing.

How is mashed potato
served in Lumpy Space?
With plenty of LUMPS.

When is the moon
at its heaviest?
When it's full.

Why didn't Finn
and Jake fit in
at Promcoming?
Their moves were
too smooth.

What does LSP
eat with stew?
Lumplings!

What holds up a moon? Moon beams!

What do you call a magician in Lumpy Space? A flying sorcerer!

What's the difference between LSP and a camel? One has lumps, the other has humps!

What's purple, lumpy and soft inside? A badly made marshmallow. And also LSP.

How do people drink tea in Lumpy Space?
With lots of sugar lumps!

LSP: Knock, knock!
Jake: Who's there?
LSP: Bean.
Jake: Bean who?
LSP: Bean a while since I last saw ya, Jakey!

How does Melissa drive LSP to Promcoming?
Quickly, to avoid ANY drama!

What do Lumpy Space Children play at school?
Lump rope!

Why was the night sky so surprised?
Because it had been star-tled!

When is Melissa's car like
the frog at the entrance
to Lumpy Space?
When it's being toad!

Which purple clouds
are best to sleep on
in Lumpy Space?
The lie-lac ones.

What's the centre of gravity?
The letter V!

Where do people in Lumpy Space park their cars?
Near parking meteors!

What do you call a starship that drips water?
A crying saucer!

How would a moon cut his hair?
Eclipse it!

What do you get if you cross a floating Lumper with a hot drink?
Zero gravi-tea!

Why did LSP float upwards to a different cloud?
Because she wanted to take the high ground!

When does the Lumpy Space King like the weather? When it's reign-ing.

Why don't Finn and Jake get hungry after being blasted into Lumpy Space? Because they've just had a big launch!

LSP: What's cooler than regular space?
Jake: I don't know.
LSP: LUMPY Space! THAT WAS SO OBVI, JAKE!

Finn: Dude, what's the best thing to do in Lumpy Space?
Jake: Leave.

What happened when Lumpy Space Princess sat on the antidote? She became Smooth Space Princess. Not cool.

When is Lumpy Space Princess not a princess? When she's Promcoming Queen.

What's LSP's favourite key on a keyboard? The SPACE bar.

What's a Lumpy Space Person's favourite drink? A soda FLOAT!

Why is Lumpy Space so cool? Because it's totally out of this world.

What does LSP put in her sandwiches? Space jam!

How does Lumpy Space Princess like her pillows? Lumpy. Duh!

How are the streets of Lumpy Space illuminated at night? By lump-light!

What happened when
the frog entrance to
Lumpy Space broke?
It got toad away!

Why is Brad
like a speedy,
spotted animal?
Because both
are cheetahs!

LSP: Hey, Finn, why do you think I
have a star on my head?

Finn: I don't know, LSP. Why?

LSP: Because I'm star-tlingly
attractive, RIGHT? RIGHT! So obvi.

Marceline's Creepy Bonus Jokes

What do you call a good-looking, friendly, kind monster?
A FAILURE.

Which monsters have the best hearing?
The eeriest.

How do skeletons start their letters?
Tomb it may concern . . .

Why did the vampire bite Finn and Jake?
Because he had a taste for adventure!

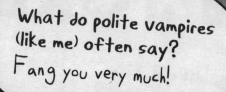

What do polite vampires (like me) often say? Fang you very much!

What happened to the monster who ate a clock? He got ticks!

Why do you never get fat vampires? Because they eat NECKS to nothing!

What's a vampire's favourite sport? Bat-minton.

FAN JOKES

What do you have if Finn and Jake get superpowers?
Avenger Time!

Kim

How do you stop a vampire from eating your fries?
Serve them with a stake and garlic salt!

Joel

Why can Jake swim so well?
Because he has a Finn!

Jessica

Where does bad light go?
To prism!

Mo

Why did Jake snap his fingers in front of Lumpy Space Princess?
Because she seemed pretty spaced out!

Brandon

Why did Jake have to cross the road?
Because he'd left his butt on the other side.
Alex

How do crazy people go through the Evil Forest?
They take the psychopath.
Rosie

Why are the people in the Mushroom Village always having parties?
Because they're fungis!
Lex

What do ghosts like for dessert?
I scream!
Noah

How does LSP like her porridge?
Lumpy!
Mia

CLOUD KINGDOM

What do you call the Party
God when he goes missing?
A where-wolf!

What did one raindrop say to its
two raindrop friends?
Two's company, but three's a cloud.

What do you call a cloud that's
too lazy to stay in the sky?
Fog!

Finn: I tried to catch
some fog earlier.
Jake: Yeah? What
happened?
Finn: I mist!

Why are Cloud People like a soggy school?
Because they're Water Elementals!

What does a rain cloud
wear under its raincoat?
Thunderwear.

What did one lightning
bolt say to the other?
You're shocking.

What did the evaporating raindrop say?
I'm just letting off some steam!

What is a Cloud
Person when they're
in the Fire Kingdom?
In trouble!

What day of the week
is the least cloudy?
Sunday.

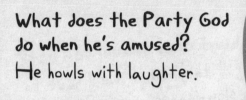

What does the Party God
do when he's amused?
He howls with laughter.

Why should you be careful
when it rains cats and dogs?
You might step in a poodle.

Why did Jake get distracted
from saving his buddy Finn?
His vision was clouded!

What kind of bow
can't be tied?
A rainbow!

Why do hurricanes travel so fast?
Because, if they didn't, we'd have to call them slow-icanes.

What's the opposite of a cold front?
A warm back!

How do hurricanes see?
With one eye!

Why did the grumpy dude bring toilet paper to the Cloud Kingdom?
Because he was a party pooper!

How does lightning
get around?
It bolts.

How easy is it for gusts of
wind to talk to each other?
It's a breeze!

How do Cloud People like
their cakes?
Light and fluffy!

Finn: Knock, knock!
Cloud Man: Who's there?
Finn: Lettuce.
Cloud Man: Lettuce who?
Finn: Lettuce into your
cloud house already!

What did the guy raindrop
say to the girl raindrop?
I'm really falling for you!

What did the dirt say to the rain?
Stop it or my name will be mud.

What did the straight-faced
cloud say to the joker cloud?
Are you being cirrus?!

What's a
Cloud Person's
favourite game?
Twister.

What is the richest
kind of air?
A million-air-e.

What do you call it when
two hurricanes fall in love?
A whirlwind romance.

What did the cloud say when
he was a little confused?
I'm sorry, my mind is a little foggy!

Where is better
to party than the
Cloud Kingdom?
NOWHERE, BRO!

Marceline's Creepy Bonus Jokes

Why did the ghost get arrested?
He didn't have a haunting licence.

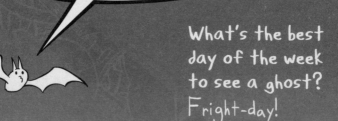

What do you get when you cross
a vampire and a school teacher?
A blood test!

What's the best
day of the week
to see a ghost?
Fright-day!

Where do vampires keep
their money?
In a blood bank!

What's my favourite game to play with Finn and Jake? Hide-and-SHRIEK!

When do vampires like to watch a race? When it's neck and neck!

What do you call a haunted chicken? A poultry-geist!

Why was the vampire heartbroken? She loved someone in vein.

Why are vampire houses such noisy places? Because of all the coffin.

FAN JOKES

Why did the man with one hand cross the road?
To get to the second-hand shop!

Rebecca

What kind of pie can fly?
A magpie!

Oliver

What do you call a fly with no wings?
A walk.

Holly

What does Marceline use to clean her hair?
Sham-BOO!

Ethan

How does the Party God greet newcomers?
Howl's it going?

James

What do you call a crazy moon?
A lunar-tic!

Rosie

What did Finn say when
he solved an equation?
MATHEMATICAL!
Sophie

What do you call the Party God when
he has his music turned up really loud?
Anything you like. He can't hear you!
James

Why is Jake's
friend not fat?
Because he's Finn!
Lewis

What does
Marceline put
on her bagels?
Scream-cheese.
Daniel

Who is the only monster better
at jokes than Marceline?
Prank-enstein.

Mateo

Finn and Jake's Best

What kind of table has no legs?
A multiplication table.

What is Tree Trunks' favourite mathematical dessert?
Apple Pi!

What would you call a world without decimals?
Pointless!

If you had eight apples in one hand and ten in the other, what would you have?
Really big hands!

Mathematical Jokes!

What did zero say to eight? Nice belt!

What do you get if you divide the circumference of a pumpkin by its diameter? Pumpkin Pi!

What shape is like a lost parrot? A poly-gon!

Why did Finn eat his maths homework? Because the teacher said it was a piece of cake.

Why are decimals so good at arguing?
Because they have a point!

How do you make seven even?
Take away the S.

Which snakes are good at sums?
Adders!

Why did the two fours skip lunch?
They already eight.

Why was the maths book sad?
Because it had too many problems!

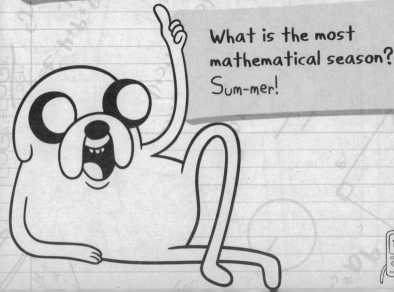

What tool can you use when doing maths?
Multi-pliers.

What sound does a mathematical clock make?
Arithma-ticks!

How do you make one vanish?
Add a G and it's gone!

What is the most mathematical season?
Sum-mer!